Acknowled

Published by Life Sports Ltd.
120 Leeds Road
Oulton
Leeds
LS26 8JY
Tel: 0113 282 4342
Fax: 0113 282 4342
E-mail: Richardh.sharp@virgin.net

Technogym UK Ltd.
Fitness and Biomedical Equipment
Suite G2
Doncastle House
Doncastle Road
Bracknell, Berkshire
RG12 8PE

ISBN-10 1-900723-01-8
ISBN-13 978-1-900723-01-5

Printed in the United Kingdom
by Interprint 0800 975 7514

Damian McGrath is a partner in "The Edge 2 Performance Ltd", along with the former England RFU coach, and Rugby League great, Joe Lydon.

They are currently working in both the business and sporting world using their experience and expertise to enhance their client's performance.

If you feel your club or organisation could benefit from the expertise Damian or Joe have to offer, whether it's a practical skills/games session or in a classroom session on topics ranging from team organisation to maximising your team's potential please contact them at the Edge 2 Perfomance Ltd.

Freephone   0800 881 8742

E-mail: damian@edge2.com

joe@edge2.com

www.theedge2.com

101 Rugby Training Drills

We would like to thank all our customers that bought the above book. We at Life Sports have been delighted by the success of this product. We have now sold over 15,000 copies over 4 editions and it has officially been given the title of the "Best Selling Rugby Coaching Book" on the market, with rave reviews from Amazon and Rugby World.

The book is still available and selling better then ever, we hope you enjoy this book just as much.

Introduction

Every coach knows that players love to play games in training. A game of 'Touch and Pass' is always clamoured for whether you're dealing with juniors or senior internationals. However, more often than not, the games play no purpose in educating or improving the players. A well organised game has many benefits, not only can it help with fitness, develop and progress skill levels, but it can, if properly used, improve a players understanding – their 'GAMESENSE' or 'GAME-AWARENESS'.

You will often see players in team games following the ball around in a group. Their individual skills may be very good but much of this is lost by the 'pack approach'. Often it needs one or two players to think about tactics and stand off the group to wait for a loose ball or a pass into space – it would provide greater opportunity. That player would have 'GAME-AWARENESS'.

'GAME-AWARENESS' can be learned. Whilst there is always a place, a very important place, for skills development and technical practices, the 'GAME-AWARENESS' method encourages players to use their basic skills as well as develop tactics and strategies themselves.

By making games a focus of a training session, rather than technical practices you can make the players take on the responsibility of finding solutions for themselves. It challenges them to think about what they are doing and why.

By asking questions and setting game related problems, coaches can promote a 'thinking approach' in players of all ages and abilities. The games and relays that follow are simple and fun, but no matter what standard the participants are, they can be won by players who can not only execute the skills required, but more importantly, work out the best way to approach them.

As with all games and drills the dimensions can be adjusted dependent on the age, size or ability of the players. I'm sure once you've got the hang of all these games you will adapt and change them to suit your needs.

Damian McGrath

1	ROB THE NEST

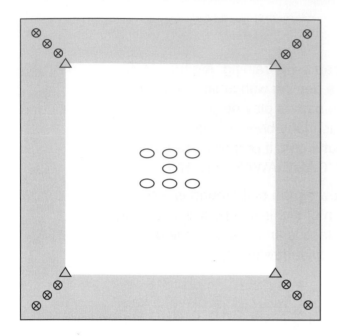

2	THIEF

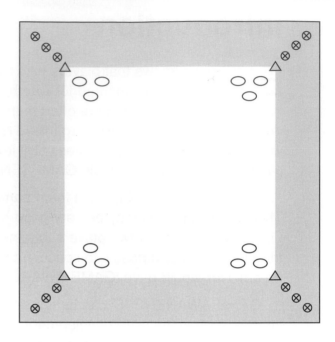

PLAYERS	4 Teams
WHAT DO YOU NEED?	7 Balls, 4 Cones
GRID SIZE	12m x 12m

○	Ball
⊗	Player
⌒	Bag
▭	Shield
------→	Kick/Roll
·········→	Run Without a Ball
———→	Pass
———→	Run With a Ball
△	Cone/Marker

PLAYERS	4 Teams
WHAT DO YOU NEED?	4/8/12 Balls, 4 Cones
GRID SIZE	12m x 12m

○	Ball
⊗	Player
⌒	Bag
▭	Shield
------→	Kick/Roll
·········→	Run Without a Ball
———→	Pass
———→	Run With a Ball
△	Cone/Marker

Explanation

- 4 teams are positioned on each corner of the grid.
- 7 balls are placed in the middle.
- On the whistle one player from each team runs to the centre and picks up a ball and returns it to their corner. He then tags the next player who repeats (player one goes to the end of the line).
- When all the balls have been taken from the centre, players can steal balls from other teams.
- The first team to have 3 balls at their corner wins.
- Only one player from each team may enter the grid at any one time and only one ball at a time may be taken.

Extension

- When a player runs to the centre of the grid for a ball he must PASS it back to the player at the front of this line (rather than run back with it).
- He then must run back and take the ball back from this player and place it on the ground.
- The next player can only go when the ball is placed on the ground.
- If the pass is not caught cleanly then the passer must retrieve the ball and replace it in the centre (or where he passed it from) and then tag the next man (ie. they lose an opportunity to score).

Explanation

- 4 teams are positioned, one on each corner.
- An equal number of balls are placed in front of each team.
- On the coaches whistle the team runs to another group and brings a ball back to their team.
- The winning group is the one with the most balls in front of them at the final whistle.

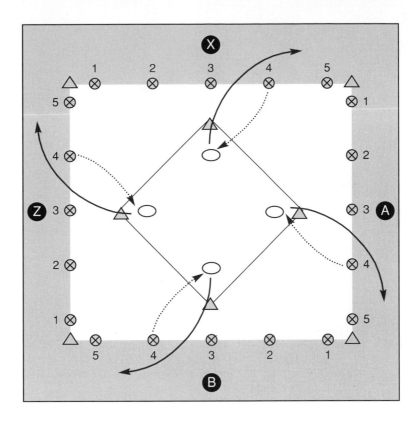

PLAYERS	4 Equal Teams
WHAT DO YOU NEED?	4 Balls, 8 Cones
GRID SIZE	Depends on Numbers, Size and Age

⬭	Ball
⊗	Player
⌒	Bag
▭	Shield
- - - ▸	Kick/Roll
·······▸	Run Without a Ball
——▸	Pass
——▸	Run With a Ball
△	Cone/Marker

Explanation

- The grid is filled by four equal teams.
- Each occupies one side of the grid facing inwards and is numbered consecutively from right to left.
- On a smaller grid inside the main grid each team places a ball.
- The coach calls a number (eg. 4) that numbered player runs forward and collects his team's ball and returns through the space he has vacated.
- He then runs to the right all the way around the grid – back in through his space to score a try in the central grid.
- First player to score gains a point for his team.

Progression

- When a player is running around the grid add such variations as 'fig 8 through legs', waist rotation, bouncing ball, dribbling ball etc.
- Run in opposite direction.

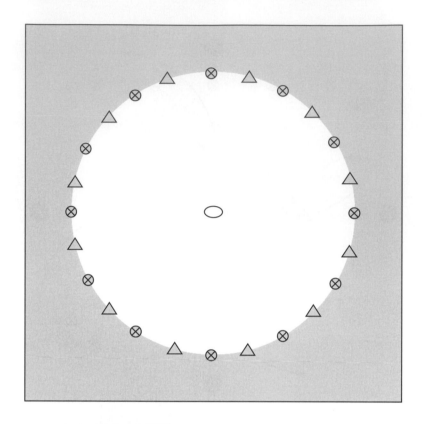

PLAYERS	Various
WHAT DO YOU NEED?	1 Ball, 12 Cones
GRID SIZE	12m Diameter Circle

◯	Ball
⊗	Player
◠	Bag
▭	Shield
- - - ▸	Kick/Roll
·······▸	Run Without a Ball
——▸	Pass
——▸	Run With a Ball
△	Cone/Marker

Explanation

- Players form a circle.
- A ball is passed around the circle in any direction.
- However it cannot be passed back to the player who passed it to them.
- A player is removed if he is in possession when the coach blows the whistle or if he throws a bad pass or fails to catch a good pass.

Progression

- Add a second ball or if very competent a third ball.

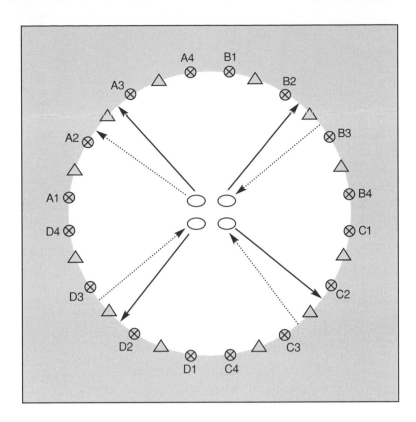

PLAYERS	4 Teams
WHAT DO YOU NEED?	4 Balls, 12 Cones
GRID SIZE	12m Diameter Circle

⬭	Ball
⊗	Player
◠	Bag
▭	Shield
- - - - ►	Kick/Roll
·········►	Run Without a Ball
——►	Pass
——►	Run With a Ball
△	Cone/Marker

Explanation

- The players form around a large circle and they are split into 4 teams.
- Each is given a number eg. 1,2,3 or 4.
- Players jog to their left around the circle.
- Each team has a ball placed in the middle of the circle.
- On the whistle the coach calls a number and that player runs out, collects a ball and brings it back to score a try over the line of the circle.
- First to score wins.

Progression

- Change direction of the runners.

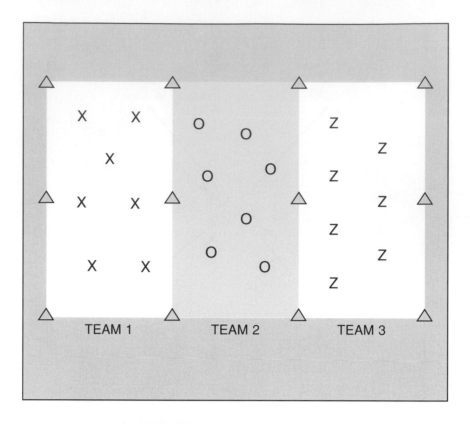

TEAM 1　　　TEAM 2　　　TEAM 3

PLAYERS	3 Teams
WHAT DO YOU NEED?	4 Balls, 12 Cones
GRID SIZE	10m x 30m

⬭	Ball
⊗	Player
⌂	Bag
▭	Shield
- - - - ➤	Kick/Roll
·········➤	Run Without a Ball
⟶	Pass
⟶	Run With a Ball
△	Cone/Marker

Explanation

- The group is divided into 3 teams – X, O, Z.
- One team is placed in each of the three boxes.
- Players can run around in their own box only (with or without the ball).
- On the whistle team 1 and team 3 attempt to pass 4 balls from one
  end to the other whilst team 2 attempt to intercept or knock down the balls or force an error from the players in team 1 and 3. (Error is dropped ball or when the ball goes out of bounds or is not caught at all).

- Players in team 1 or 3 must not hold the ball for longer than 3 seconds.
- If a ball is dropped/missed/intercepted etc. it is removed from the game.
- At the end of the allotted time, the number of balls left is the score for the MIDDLE TEAM (ie. team 2).
- Reverse roles, team with highest score is the winner.

Extension

- Add more balls
- Kicking instead of passing

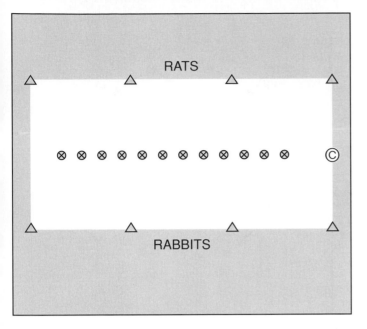

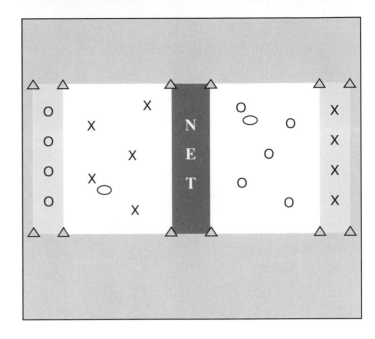

PLAYERS	Squad
WHAT DO YOU NEED?	8 Cones
GRID SIZE	10m x 30m (longer if more players)

	Ball
⊗	Player
⌂	Bag
▭	Shield
-------→	Kick/Roll
·············→	Run Without a Ball
———→	Pass
———→	Run With a Ball
△	Cone/Marker

Explanation

- Players stand in the centre of the grid facing the coach (©).
- Coach shouts either 'Rats' or 'Rabbits' and the players react to the called name by running to that side and returning to <u>sit</u> in the middle where they started from.
- Last man back is eliminated.
- The game finishes when only one person is left.

PLAYERS	2 Teams
WHAT DO YOU NEED?	2 Balls, 12 Cones
GRID SIZE	10m x 30m

	Ball
⊗	Player
⌂	Bag
▭	Shield
-------→	Kick/Roll
·············→	Run Without a Ball
———→	Pass
———→	Run With a Ball
△	Cone/Marker

Explanation

- Split the players into 2 teams.
- Each team is given a ball.
- Players from each team stand in the 'channel' at the far end of the grid from their own players.
- To score a point the ball must be passed over the net and the opposition players to be caught on the full by the players in the channel.
- No player can step out of his channel to catch or pass the ball.
- The opposition attempt to knock it down or intercept.
- If intercepted the 'channel' player retrieves the ball.
- If successful the player who passed it and the player who caught it change places.
- 1pt for each successful catch.
- First team to score 20pts wins.

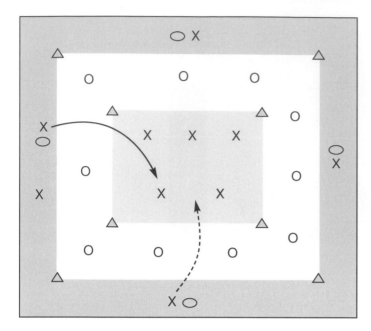

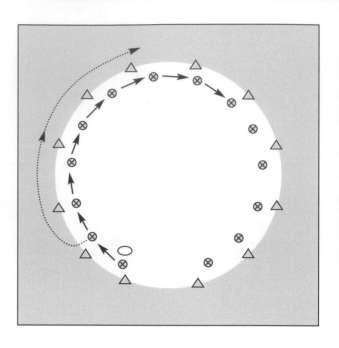

PLAYERS	2 Teams
WHAT DO YOU NEED?	4 Balls, 8 Cones
GRID SIZE	20m x 20m (large) 10m x 10m (small)

PLAYERS	As required
WHAT DO YOU NEED?	1 Ball, 12 Cones
GRID SIZE	Depends on players Size and Age

⬭	Ball
⊗	Player
⌂	Bag
▭	Shield
------→	Kick/Roll
·······→	Run Without a Ball
——→	Pass
——→	Run With a Ball
△	Cone/Marker

⬭	Ball
⊗	Player
⌂	Bag
▭	Shield
------→	Kick/Roll
·······→	Run Without a Ball
——→	Pass
——→	Run With a Ball
△	Cone/Marker

Explanation

- 2 grids are set up with a small grid inside a large one.
- The players are split into 2 teams.
- Team B (O) are defenders whilst team A (X) are the attackers.
- Team A are split so that one group are 'marooned' on the small grid and one group are on the outside of the large grid with the 4 balls.
- On the coaches whistle team A players on the outside attempt to kick or pass the ball to the players 'marooned' in the middle.
- These players must catch the ball on the full and not step outside the small grid.
- They then return the ball back to their players on the outside.
- Team A players can move around with the ball but cannot be in possession for more than 5 seconds.
- Team B players are allowed to run around their area but not leave it. They try to intercept or distract the passers/kickers/catchers.
- Everytime a ball is dropped or intercepted or hits the ground that ball is removed.
- At the end of 2 minutes the whistle goes and points are given for the number of balls left.
- Roles are then reversed.

Explanation

- Players form on the outside of the circle.
- One player has a ball.
- On the coaches whistle the ball is passed all around the circle to the left.
- As soon as player 2 has passed to player 3 he runs around the circle to the right (ie. in the opposite direction) and tries to get back in position before the ball gets back there.
- When the ball gets back to its original start position the runner must stop.
- The coach gives him a score for how many players in the circle he ran past.

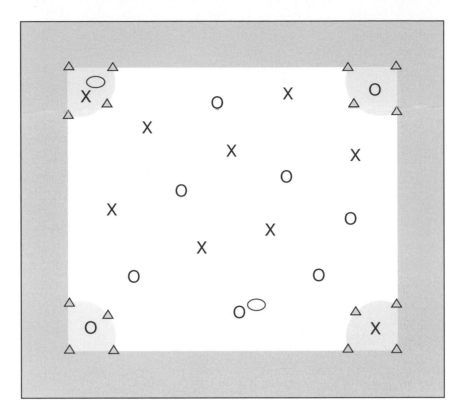

PLAYERS	2 Teams
WHAT DO YOU NEED?	2 Balls, 16 Cones
GRID SIZE	Depends on Numbers, Size and Age

◯	Ball
⊗	Player
◠	Bag
▭	Shield
- - - - - ▶	Kick/Roll
· · · · · · ▶	Run Without a Ball
——▶	Pass
——▶	Run With a Ball
△	Cone/Marker

Explanation

- Divide your players into two equal teams.
- Give each team a ball (The ball is placed in one of the neutral corners when the team being chased is not using it).
- Team A (O) begins using their ball to tag team B (X).
- On the whistle team A attempt to tig team B with the ball.
- They <u>MUST</u> have the ball in 2 hands when they tag the player.
- They cannot run with the ball in their possession but they can take a step when trying to tig someone.
- Each time a player is tagged team A score a point, the player who is tagged stays in the game, as no one is eliminated.
- No player can be tagged consecutively by team A.

- Team B can use their diagonally opposite safety corners to briefly rest players but only one player at a time is allowed in there.
- After 2 mins the teams change around on the coaches whistle.
- The team A player in possession puts his team's ball in one of the their corners while a player from team B retrieves his ball and the game immediately continues.
- There is no break in play, team B straight away tries to tag team A.
- The coach continuously changes roles throughout and keeps adding up the scores. Both teams should get equal time.

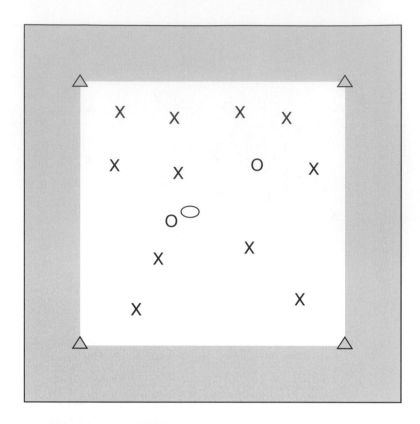

PLAYERS	Squad
WHAT DO YOU NEED?	1 Ball, 4 Cones
GRID SIZE	15m x 15m

◯	Ball
⊗	Player
◠	Bag
▭	Shield
- - - -➤	Kick/Roll
·······➤	Run Without a Ball
——➤	Pass
——➤	Run With a Ball
△	Cone/Marker

Explanation

- 2 chasers try to tig the other players with a ball (The ball must be held in 2 hands).
- When touched, that player must stand still (ie. 'turn to cement').
- That player can be released by another player touching him below the knee with both hands.
- Chasers can run with the ball and are allowed to pass it between them.
- After 90 seconds the coach blows the whistle and counts the number of players who are 'cement'.
- Points are given for each one.
- Any players who bump into each other must also turn to 'cement' and all players must remain in the grid.

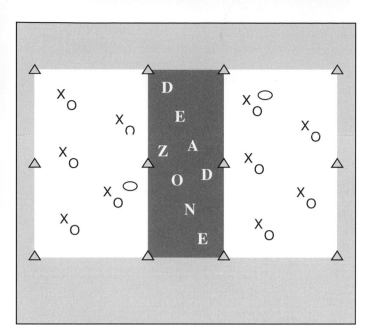

PLAYERS	20
WHAT DO YOU NEED?	1 Ball, 12 Cones
GRID SIZE	10m x 20m

⬭	Ball
⊗	Player
⌒	Bag
▭	Shield
------▸	Kick/Roll
┄┄┄▸	Run Without a Ball
──▸	Pass
──▸	Run With a Ball
△	Cone/Marker

Explanation
- Split the players into 2 groups (X and O).
- Place half of each team in the 2 end grids leaving a 'dead' zone in the middle.
- X's begin with the ball.
- They try to pass the ball across the 'dead zone' to a member of their own team who is in a good position to receive it.
- The O's attempt to intercept or knock down the passes or force the X's to drop the ball. <u>BUT</u> <u>NO</u> <u>CONTACT</u> is allowed.
- X's cannot run with the ball nor hold it for longer than 3 seconds.
- Every pass caught is one point for the team.
- Everytime a pass is dropped/intercepted etc. possession changes.
- Team with highest score is the winner.

Extension
- Add more balls.

PLAYERS	2 Teams
WHAT DO YOU NEED?	2 Balls, 10 Cones
GRID SIZE	10m x 20m

⬭	Ball
⊗	Player
⌒	Bag
▭	Shield
------▸	Kick/Roll
┄┄┄▸	Run Without a Ball
──▸	Pass
──▸	Run With a Ball
△	Cone/Marker

Explanation
- Split the players into 2 equal teams (X and O).
- Each team nominates a kicker and a full back.
- The players from each team lie prone 5m from the half way line facing each other with their nominated kicker in behind and their full back placed where they wish.
- The kicker has the ball at their feet.
- On the coach's whistle the kicker picks up the ball and kicks the ball as far into opposition territory as possible.
- The balls are collected by the respective full backs who must drop to their knees until <u>all</u> their team mates are behind the ball.
- As soon as their team mates are 'onside' they can pass to any one of them.
- All the players must handle at least once before the last man scores a try back at the half way line.
- First team to score collects a point for their team.
- The teams can attempt to charge down the opposition kicker if they wish.
- The kicker must keep the ball in the field of play.

Extension
- Have the ball passed to the kicker on the coach's whistle rather than picking it up and kicking it.
- Instead of having the players prone – get them to shuttle back and forth over 3m until the coach blows his whistle.

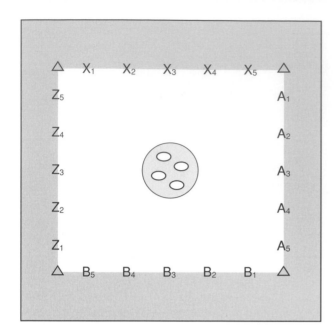

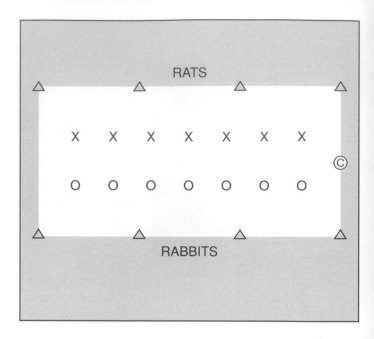

PLAYERS	20
WHAT DO YOU NEED?	4 Ball, 4 Cones
GRID SIZE	Depends on Numbers, Size and Age

⬭	Ball
⊗	Player
⌒	Bag
▭	Shield
- - - -→	Kick/Roll
········→	Run Without a Ball
——→	Pass
——→	Run With a Ball
△	Cone/Marker

PLAYERS	2 Teams
WHAT DO YOU NEED?	8 Cones (tag belts optional)
GRID SIZE	20m x 40m (dependant on numbers)

⬭	Ball
⊗	Player
⌒	Bag
▭	Shield
- - - -→	Kick/Roll
········→	Run Without a Ball
——→	Pass
——→	Run With a Ball
△	Cone/Marker

Explanation

- The grid is filled with four equal teams.
- Each occupies one side of the grid facing inwards and is numbered consecutively from right to left.
- A plastic bin or large box (or if needs be a small 'coned' square) is placed in the middle of the large square and in it each team places a ball.
- The coach calls a number and that designated player runs to the centre of the grid and collects his team's ball.
- The ball is brought back and placed at player 1's feet.
- The player who retrieved the ball returns to his place.
- As soon as he is in position the ball is passed from player 1 to player 2 etc to the end of the line and back to player 1 (all players must handle).
- As soon as the ball is back to player 1 the player who collected the ball from the middle returns it back there.
- First team to do so scores a point.

Progression

- Change the skill from normal passing to overhead passing, one handed passing, kicking or make each player do a 'figure of 8' or waist rotation before handing on.

Explanation

- Split players into 2 equal groups.
- Stand them, arms length apart in 2 lines down the corridor facing the coach (©).
- X are the 'Rats' and O are the 'Rabbits'.
- The coach calls 'Rats' or 'Rabbits' and that team must attempt to get over their line without being tagged by the other team.
- If a player is tagged he is eliminated.
- The team with the most players left after 2 minutes is the winner.

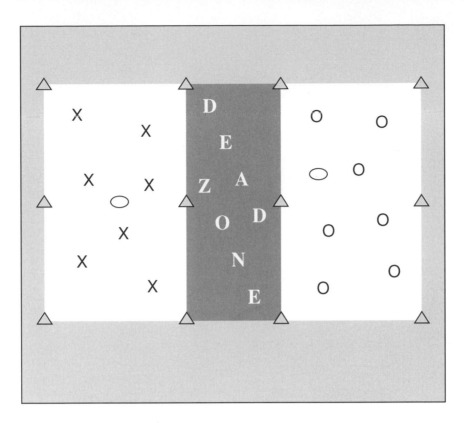

PLAYERS	2 Teams
WHAT DO YOU NEED?	2 Balls, 12 Cones
GRID SIZE	10m x 30m

⬭	Ball
⊗	Player
◠	Bag
▭	Shield
- - - - - →	Kick/Roll
············→	Run Without a Ball
———→	Pass
———→	Run With a Ball
△	Cone/Marker

Explanation

- Split the players into 2 teams.
- One at each end.
- Balls can only be passed rugby style and players must catch and pass instantly (ie. 2 seconds).
- The ball can be passed to someone on your side before it is passed across to the opposition.
- A maximum of 3 people only can touch it before it must be passed back.
- The aim is to force an error from the opposition (eg. drop pass, pass out-of-bounds) which gives your team a point.
- The game is played until one team scores 10pts.

Extension

- Play as elimination ie. players making errors are out of the game, and the team with the most players left at the end of the allotted time are the winners.

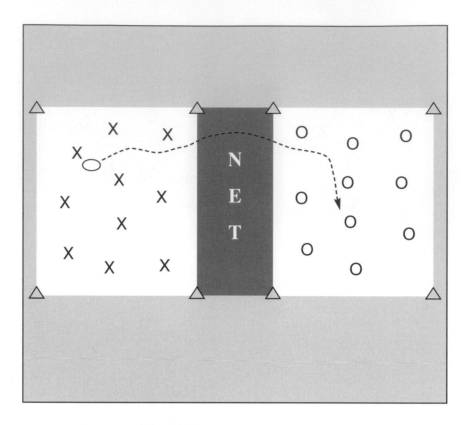

PLAYERS	2 Teams
WHAT DO YOU NEED?	1 Balls, 8 Cones
GRID SIZE	10m x 30m

⬭	Ball
⊗	Player
⌂	Bag
▭	Shield
- - - - ➤	Kick/Roll
·············➤	Run Without a Ball
——➤	Pass
——➤	Run With a Ball
△	Cone/Marker

Explanation

- Split the players into 2 equal sides.

- The teams stand either side of the area marked 'Net'.

- The ball must go at least 6 feet in height as well as clearing the 'Net'.

- The team with the ball kicks the ball over the 'Net' attempting to bounce it in the oppositions grid.

- The receivers attempt to catch it before it bounces.

- If they do (the kickers can put up high bombs to pressure the defenders into dropping the ball) they can kick it back to try and bounce it in the other grid.

- If a receiver drops the ball he is out and leaves the game.

- If a kick bounces in the grid successfully, the receiver nearest where the ball bounces is out and leaves the game.

- If a player kicks the ball out of bounds on the full, or underneath the 6ft rule or into the 'Net' he is out and leaves the game.

- The team which loses all their players loses the game .

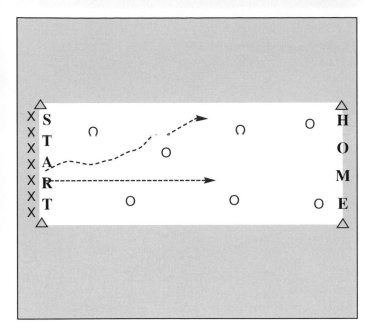

PLAYERS	2 Teams
WHAT DO YOU NEED?	1 Ball, 4 Cones
GRID SIZE	20m x 50m

⬭	Ball
⊗	Player
⌂	Bag
▭	Shield
- - - - - ►	Kick/Roll
·············►	Run Without a Ball
──────►	Pass
──────►	Run With a Ball
△	Cone/Marker

Explanation

- Split the players into 2 teams.
- One team (X) are the kickers the other team (O) are fielders.
- One at a time, The kicking team have to kick the ball into open space and run through the grid (No Man's Land) and get safely to Home.
- A player is out if the fielders catch the ball on the full or having fielded the ball they tig the kickers inside No Man's Land. (They may pass or kick the ball to each other and they can run with the ball).
- A point is given each time a player gets 'Home'.
- Once there have been three players out the teams change places.
- The kicker must kick the ball inside No Mans Land from behind the 'start' line.

PLAYERS	2 Teams
WHAT DO YOU NEED?	2 Balls, 26 Cones
GRID SIZE	10m x 30m

⬭	Ball
⊗	Player
⌂	Bag
▭	Shield
- - - - - ►	Kick/Roll
·············►	Run Without a Ball
──────►	Pass
──────►	Run With a Ball
△	Cone/Marker

Explanation

- Split the players into 2 equal sides.
- Line them up single file facing up the corridor on opposite sides of the grid.
- On the whistle, the front player from each team runs in and out of the cones, zig-zag style, up the corridor.
- On rounding the end cone they then race back collect a ball and score back over the line.
- First player to do so successfully scores a point for their team.
- The balls are then replaced in a different position for the next players.

Extension

- Coach (or nominated rollers) rolls in the balls after the players have rounded the last cone.

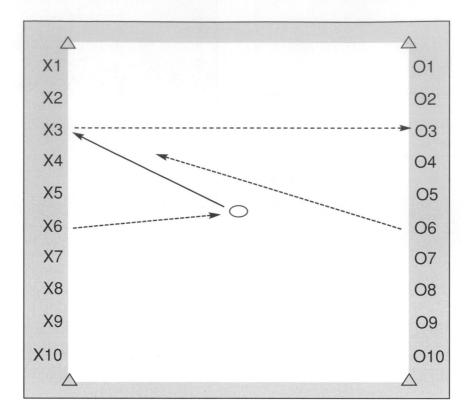

PLAYERS	2 Teams
WHAT DO YOU NEED?	1 Ball, 4 Cones
GRID SIZE	20m x 20m

◯	Ball
⊗	Player
⌒	Bag
▭	Shield
- - - - -▶	Kick/Roll
·····▶	Run Without a Ball
——▶	Pass
——▶	Run With a Ball
△	Cone/Marker

Explanation

- Split the players into 2 teams and give each a number.
- The players are lined up facing each other on both sides of the corridor.
- The coach calls a number the player from each team with that number runs forward and attempts to get the ball.
- In order to return it to his team the successful player, on gaining possession, passes the ball to anyone on his team.
- That player must grubber kick the ball and attempt to get it through the oppositions line.

- The player who does not win possession of the ball in the middle can try and put pressure on the kicker.
- His team mates try and defend their line by remaining on their line and attempting to catch the grubber kick.
- One point is allotted for each successful kick.
- The game then is reset to begin again.

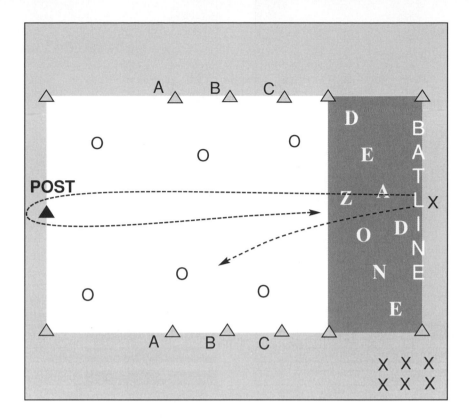

PLAYERS	2 Teams
WHAT DO YOU NEED?	1 Ball, 13 Cones
GRID SIZE	Various

⬭	Ball
⊗	Player
⌒	Bag
▭	Shield
------➤	Kick/Roll
·······➤	Run Without a Ball
——➤	Pass
——➤	Run With a Ball
△	Cone/Marker
▲	Red Post Cone

Explanation

- Split the players into 2 equal sides, one team (X) bats and the other (O) fields.

- The batsman stands behind the 'bat line' and has a 3m area in front of him in which is the 'dead zone'.

- The batter can grubber kick the ball anywhere in the corridor (it must stay in play) but not into the 'dead zone'.

- As soon as he has kicked it the batter must run around the 'Post Cone' at the far end and get back over the bat line to score a run.

- If the ball is caught on the full or goes out of the grid he is out.

- He can be 'run-out' if the fielders collect the ball and pass the ball to a man on the 'post' at the far end and he must pass it to fielders who take up positions on cones A, B & C on either side. 'C' must pass the ball to a fielder on the 'Bat Line' before the batsman crosses it.

- After 3 players are out the teams swap roles.

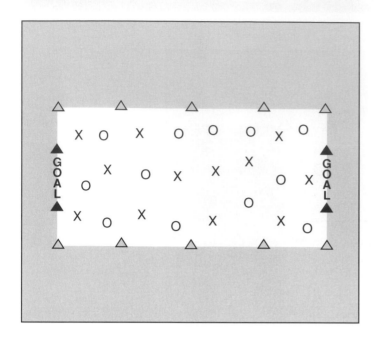

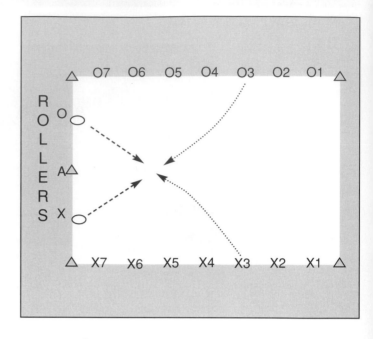

PLAYERS	2 Teams
WHAT DO YOU NEED?	1 Ball, 14 Cones
GRID SIZE	Varies on numbers

PLAYERS	2 Teams
WHAT DO YOU NEED?	2 Balls, 12 Cones
GRID SIZE	10m x 26m

⬭	Ball
⊗	Player
⬠	Bag
▭	Shield
- - - - -➤	Kick/Roll
·······➤	Run Without a Ball
——➤	Pass
——➤	Run With a Ball
△	Cone/Marker
▲	Red Post Cone

⬭	Ball
⊗	Player
⬠	Bag
▭	Shield
- - - - -➤	Kick/Roll
·······➤	Run Without a Ball
——➤	Pass
——➤	Run With a Ball
△	Cone/Marker

Explanation

- Split the players into 2 equal teams.
- An equal number of players are placed in each area (as above) and cannot move from that area.
- The game begins with a 'tap kick on the half-way line.
- Each team is allocated 6 tackles (each new tackle begins with a 'tap kick').
- The attacking team can run, pass or kick the ball in any direction to their team mates in other zones.
- The aim is to grubber kick the ball between the goals, each goal scored is worth 1 point.
- The ball changes to the other team when the team in possession are i) 'tigged' on the 6th tackle
   ii) The ball is kicked or passed over the sideline or baseline
   iii) The ball is Knocked-on
   iv) The ball is intercepted by the opposition.

Explanation

- Split the players into 2 teams and give each member a number.
- Stand each team on either side of the grid facing their opposite number.
- One player from each team is nominated as the roller and given a rugby ball.
- On the whistle the coach calls out a number and the rollers, roll out a ball to that member of the opposite team (X's roll to O's and vice versa).
- The players who are nominated must pick up the rolling ball, run around cone 'A' (between the rollers) then place the ball at the feet of player 1 on their team and return to their position.
- As soon as the nominated player is back in position the ball is passed down the line to the end man.
- First team to get the ball to the end successfully wins a point.
- Any mistakes in passing the ball must return to player 1.
- Change the 'roller' on a regular basis.

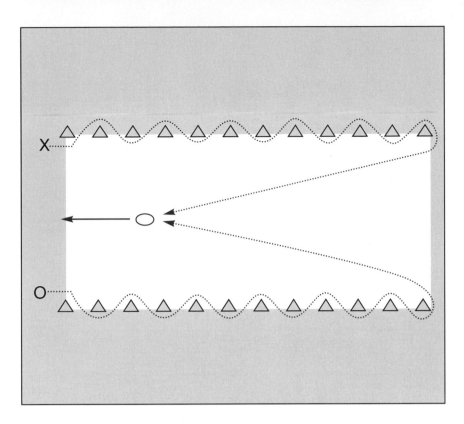

PLAYERS	2 Teams
WHAT DO YOU NEED?	1 Ball, 24 Cones
GRID SIZE	10m x 30m

◯	Ball
⊗	Player
◠	Bag
▭	Shield
- - - - -➤	Kick/Roll
·······➤	Run Without a Ball
———➤	Pass
——➤	Run With a Ball
△	Cone/Marker

Explanation

- Split the players into 2 equal teams.
- Line them up in single file Facing the corridor on opposite sides of the grid.
- The ball is placed randomly in the grid.
- On the whistle the front player from both teams runs in and out of the cones (zig zag style) up the corridor.
- On rounding the last cone they sprint back down the corridor.
- Both players try to collect the ball and score over the try line.
- No contact is allowed.

- The player without the ball can stop his opponent from scoring by two-handed tagging him or tackling him.
- A point is scored if a player scores successfully.

Extension

- As players run forward the coach rolls the ball down the corridor.

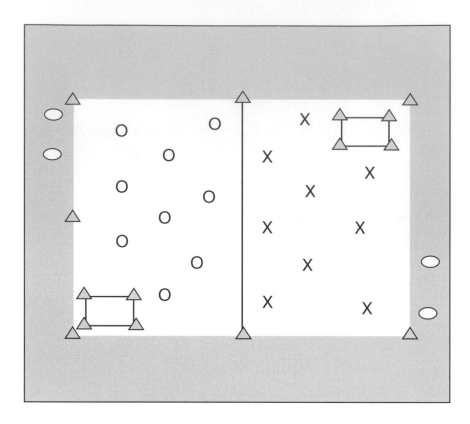

PLAYERS	2 Teams
WHAT DO YOU NEED?	4 Balls, 14 Cones
GRID SIZE	60m x 40m

⬭	Ball
⊗	Player
⌓	Bag
▭	Shield
- - - - →	Kick/Roll
·······→	Run Without a Ball
——→	Pass
——→	Run With a Ball
△	Cone/Marker

Explanation

- Split the players into 2 teams and divide the corridor into two halfs with a square prison 'Alcatraz' is marked in the back right hand corner of each half.
- 2 balls are placed 5m outside the end lines and at least 5m apart.
- On the coaches whistle the players venture into the oppositions territory to either grab a ball or release a prisoner from 'Alcatraz'.
- If a player reaches a ball from behind the oppositions line without being touched then he is allowed to walk free with the ball to place it alongside the balls behind his own line (at least 5m from them).

- If a player is touched in the oppositions half he goes to prison in their half.
- A player can be released from prison by a player reaching the prison 'untouched' the longest serving prisoner is released and both can return to their own half untouched.
- The first team to have all 4 balls in their possession wins or the team with the most balls at the end of 4 mins wins.

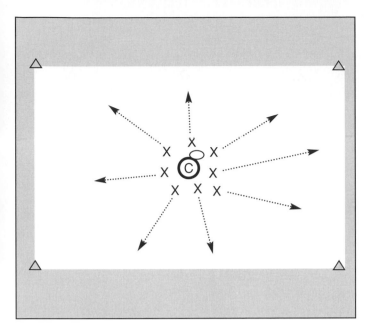

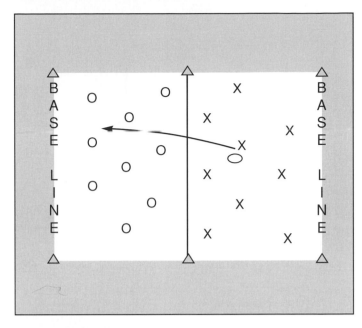

PLAYERS	10
WHAT DO YOU NEED?	1 Ball, 4 Cones
GRID SIZE	Dependant on No. of players

Ball	Ball
Player	Player
Bag	Bag
Shield	Shield
Kick/Roll	Kick/Roll
Run Without a Ball	Run Without a Ball
Pass	Pass
Run With a Ball	Run With a Ball
Cone/Marker	Cone/Marker

PLAYERS	2 Teams
WHAT DO YOU NEED?	1 Balls, 6 Cones
GRID SIZE	Depends on skill/age/size

Ball	Ball
Player	Player
Bag	Bag
Shield	Shield
Kick/Roll	Kick/Roll
Run Without a Ball	Run Without a Ball
Pass	Pass
Run With a Ball	Run With a Ball
Cone/Marker	Cone/Marker

Explanation

- All Players are given a number.
- The coach holds the ball in the middle of the grid, surrounded by all the players.
- The coach kicks/throws the ball high into the air and all the players scatter away from the ball.
- After he has kicked/thrown the ball he shouts a number.
- The player with that number, tries to catch the ball.
- As soon as he has caught it he calls "freeze" and all the other players must stand still.
- He then attempts to grubber kick the ball to hit one of the other players.
- The players cannot leave the confines of the grid.
- Players who are hit with the ball are eliminated.
- If the catcher, catches the ball on the full he can take two steps forward.
- If he misses the catch, he must take 2 steps backwards.

Explanation

- Split the players into 2 teams and divide the grid into two halves each team stands in their own grid.
- Team X begins with the ball in the middle of their grid.
- The player with the ball throws/passes (must be with two hands) as far as he can into the oppositions grid.
- As soon as one of the opponents touches it the ball is dead.
- Team O then returns the ball from this position.
- If the ball is caught on the full (i.e. without bouncing) then the player that catches it can take 2 steps towards his opponents line.
- The aim of the game is to pass the ball over your opponents base line without any of them touching it.
- A point is awarded for each success.

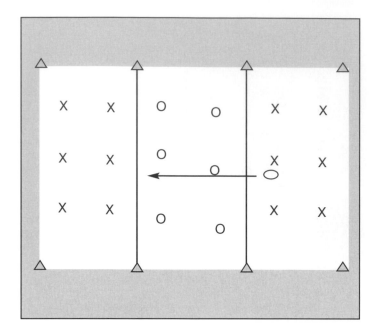

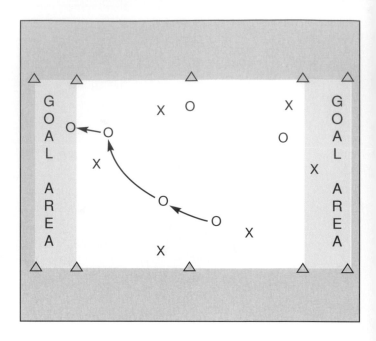

PLAYERS	Various
WHAT DO YOU NEED?	2 Balls, 8 Cones
GRID SIZE	45m x 15m

⬯	Ball
⊗	Player
⌂	Bag
▭	Shield
- - - - - - ▶	Kick/Roll
· · · · · · · ▶	Run Without a Ball
——————▶	Pass
——————▶	Run With a Ball
△	Cone/Marker

PLAYERS	2 Teams
WHAT DO YOU NEED?	1 Balls, 10 Cones
GRID SIZE	20m x 40m

⬯	Ball
⊗	Player
⌂	Bag
▭	Shield
- - - - - - ▶	Kick/Roll
· · · · · · · ▶	Run Without a Ball
——————▶	Pass
——————▶	Run With a Ball
△	Cone/Marker

Explanation

- Split the players into 3 equal groups and place each group into one of the 3 grids.
- The aim of the game is for the players in the end two grids to pass the ball and hit one or more players in the middle grid.
- The players in the middle grid try to evade the ball.
- A point is awarded when the player/players are hit by the ball.
- Each team occupies the middle grid for 3 mins.
- The end players must stay in their grids.
- The team with the least number of points against them after being in the middle wins.

Explanation

- Split the players into 2 teams.
- Each team passes the ball amongst it's own players in any direction.
- The object is to pass the ball to one of your team-mates who is standing in the oppositions 'Goal Area'.
- Only one player is allowed in their opponents Goal area at any time.
- If the ball is dropped possession changes to the other team.
- If the ball touches the floor possession changes to the other team.
- No contact is allowed, but blocking is.
- The player in possession can pass with one or two hands, but must pass with their back foot on the ground.
- Once they have passed they are free to run anywhere in the grid.
- If the ball is intercepted it is play on.
- The game begins on the baseline of the attacking team.

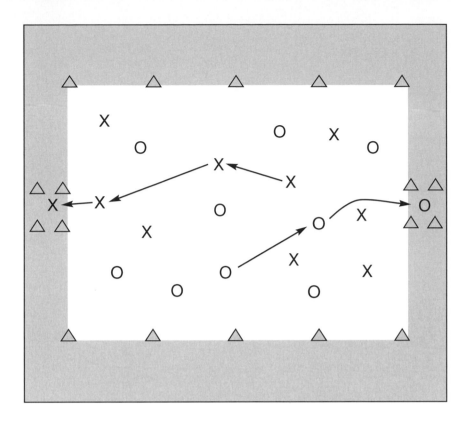

PLAYERS	2 Teams
WHAT DO YOU NEED?	1 Ball, 18 Cones, 2 Chairs/Stools
GRID SIZE	20m x 40m

⬭	Ball
⊗	Player
⌒	Bag
▭	Shield
- - - - -▶	Kick/Roll
·············▶	Run Without a Ball
──────▶	Pass
─────▶	Run With a Ball
△	Cone/Marker

Explanation

- Split the players into 2 teams.

- One player from each team is nominated as the 'basket', they stand on a chair/stool at the end of the grid and must catch a pass from their team to score a point.

- Players may run with the ball but if two hand touched by an opponent possession changes to the other team.

- A player in danger of being touched may stop and cannot be touched however after stopping he cannot begin to run again and must pass within 5 seconds or lose possession to the other team.

- The ball going to ground does not effect play, possession goes to the team who regains the ball.

- No players except the 'Basket' man is allowed inside the square around the chair/stool.

- Players can pass in any direction.

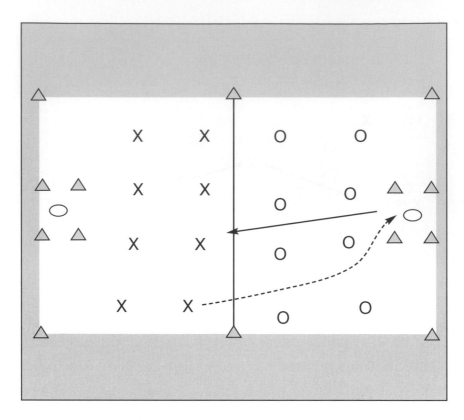

PLAYERS	2 Teams
WHAT DO YOU NEED?	2 Balls, 14 Cones
GRID SIZE	Depending on player numbers

◯	Ball
⊗	Player
◠	Bag
▭	Shield
------→	Kick/Roll
·········→	Run Without a Ball
——→	Pass
——→	Run With a Ball
△	Cone/Marker

Explanation

- Split the players into 2 equal teams.

- The grid is split into two halfs with a 'prison' marked out at each end.

- Team 'X' is on one half whilst team 'O' is on the other.

- The teams may cross into the other area at any time.

- Each team tries to steal the ball from the oppositions prison.

- A player is safe when running without the ball and when inside the prison, until he touches the ball then he can be touched by the opposition.

- If a player is touched in possession he and his team return the ball to the prison and go back to their own half before becoming live again.

- The aim is for one team to get the ball back across the half way line by chain passing and running without being touched by the opposition.

- First team to get the ball over the half way line are the winners.

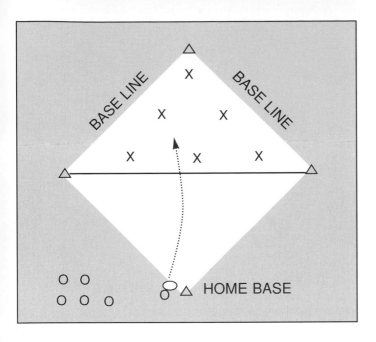

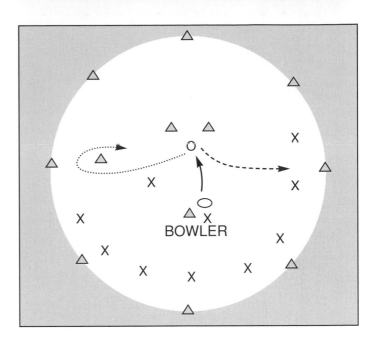

PLAYERS	2 Teams
WHAT DO YOU NEED?	1 Ball, 4 Cones,
GRID SIZE	Depends on players

◯	Ball
⊗	Player
◠	Bag
▭	Shield
--------→	Kick/Roll
···········→	Run Without a Ball
——→	Pass
——→	Run With a Ball
△	Cone/Marker

PLAYERS	2 Teams
WHAT DO YOU NEED?	1 Ball, 20 Cones
GRID SIZE	40m diameter

◯	Ball
⊗	Player
◠	Bag
▭	Shield
--------→	Kick/Roll
···········→	Run Without a Ball
——→	Pass
——→	Run With a Ball
△	Cone/Marker

Explanation

- Split the players into 2 equal teams, one team bats (O), one team field (X).
- The field is marked out as in the diagram with all the fielders spread out in the top triangle. They are not allowed to leave this area.
- On the Coach's whistle the batter kicks the ball attempting to get it over the 'Baseline'. He can use any type of kick but the ball must touch the ground in the fielder's triangle at least once.
- If the batter does this successfully he receives a point.
- If he kicks the ball out on the full or kicks the ball outside the Diamond or the ball is caught by the fielding team he is out.
- Fielders must catch or field the ball with their hands only.
- Fielders are not allowed to push, kick or block the ball to prevent it going over the baseline.
- 3 players out and the teams change roles.

Explanation

- Split the players into 2 teams.
- The grid is marked out as above.
- One team (X) are the fielders and one team (O) are the batters.
- The bowler stands 10m away from the 2 cones which act as wickets.
- He bowls by passing or kicking the ball straight at the batsman (each bowler has 6 balls per over).
- The batsman must catch the ball and then pass or kick the ball into the outfield.
- The ball must not go outside the field of play on the full.
- The batsman can be caught, run out or bowled.
- The fielding team must return the ball to the bowler who is then free to bowl again.
- The batsman after passing/kicking the ball must run around the cone (15m away) and return before the bowler can bowl again.

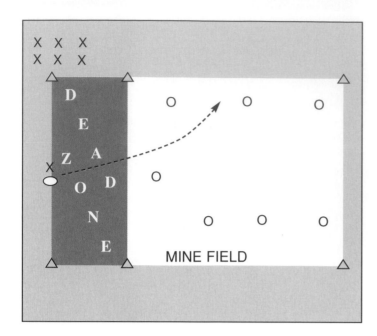

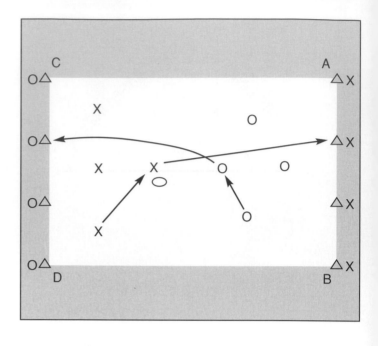

PLAYERS	2 Teams
WHAT DO YOU NEED?	1 Ball, 6 Cones,
GRID SIZE	20m x 40m

⬭	Ball
⊗	Player
⌒	Bag
▭	Shield
------>	Kick/Roll
·······>	Run Without a Ball
——>	Pass
⭢	Run With a Ball
△	Cone/Marker

PLAYERS	2 Teams of 4
WHAT DO YOU NEED?	1 Ball, 8 Cones
GRID SIZE	10m x 20m

⬭	Ball
⊗	Player
⌒	Bag
▭	Shield
------>	Kick/Roll
·······>	Run Without a Ball
——>	Pass
⭢	Run With a Ball
△	Cone/Marker

Explanation

- Split the players into 2 equal teams, one team as kickers (X), one team are catchers (O).

- The aim of the game is for the kickers to kick the ball over the 'Dead Zone' and make it land (bounce) in the minefield area where the catchers are spread out.

- If they are successful a point is scored.

- The kicking team has 3 lives

- A life is lost when a kicker kicks the ball out of bounds (first bounce) or the catching team catches the ball on the full.

- When 3 lives are lost the teams change roles.

Explanation

- Split the players into 2 teams of 4.

- X's begin in possession, they can pass forwards or backwards but it must be rugby style passes below head-height.

- They attempt to score by passing the ball to a player stood on any one of the four cones on line A-B.

- When the O's are in possession they attempt to pass the ball in the same manner to any of their players stood on any one of the cones on line C-D.

- If a player is touched in possession he must place the ball on the floor for the opposition.

- The opposition cannot be touched until a pass is made, unless someone picks it up runs immediately.

- The first team to score 10 points wins.

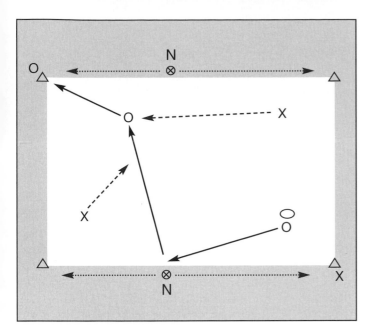

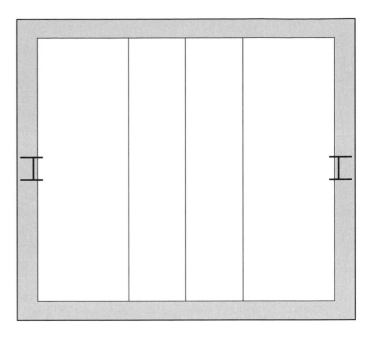

PLAYERS	2 Teams
WHAT DO YOU NEED?	1 Ball, 4 Cones,
GRID SIZE	20m x 10m

⬭	Ball
⊗	Player
⌒	Bag
▭	Shield
------→	Kick/Roll
·········→	Run Without a Ball
——→	Pass
——→	Run With a Ball
△	Cone/Marker

PLAYERS	2 Teams
WHAT DO YOU NEED?	1 Ball
GRID SIZE	Full Pitch

⬭	Ball
⊗	Player
⌒	Bag
▭	Shield
------→	Kick/Roll
·········→	Run Without a Ball
——→	Pass
——→	Run With a Ball
△	Cone/Marker

Explanation

- Teams are split into 2 teams of 3 and 2 (N) neutral players.
- A nominated player from each team stands on diagonally opposite corners.
- O's begin with possession.
- A player in possession CANNOT run with the ball.
- O's try to get the ball using rugby style (under head height) passes to their man standing on the corner.
- They can use the two neutral players (N) who can move anywhere along the sideline when not in possession
- The Neutral players play for which ever team is in possession but only stay on the sideline.
- The defenders can try to intercept passes or knock them down.
- After a mistake or a score, possession changes to the other team.
- First team to score 10 points wins.
- Passes can be forwards or backwards.

Explanation

- Split the players into 2 equal teams.
- The coach begins the game by bouncing the ball on the centre spot, whichever team collects it is in possession.
- There is NO contact.
- A player can run with the ball but approximately every three steps he must either kick and regather or bounce and regather before continuing.
- The ball can be passed or kicked to a team mate.
- If a player is touched in possession he must stop and hand over the ball to the opposition.
- If a player stands still he cannot be touched but he must pass within 3 seconds (he cannot start running again).
- If a player drops a pass or spills the ball whilst running, possession is handed over.
- To score a player must kick the ball over the posts to land (or be caught by a team mate) in the in goal area.
- First team to score 5 goals wins.

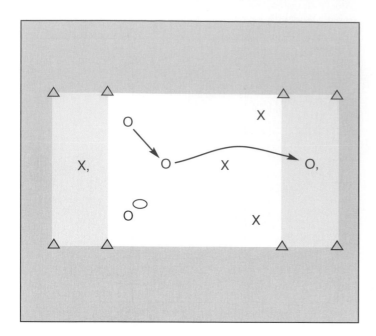

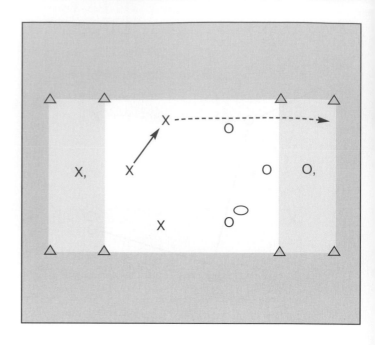

PLAYERS	2 Teams
WHAT DO YOU NEED?	1 Ball, 8 Cones,
GRID SIZE	10m x 20m

◯	Ball	
⊗	Player	
◠	Bag	
▭	Shield	
- - - - -➤	Kick/Roll	
·········➤	Run Without a Ball	
────➤	Pass	
────➤	Run With a Ball	
△	Cone/Marker	

Explanation

- Split the players into 2 teams of 4.

- The team in possession aim to get the ball to their player who is in the End Zone (shaded area) X, is the X's man and O, for the O's (they cannot leave the end zone).

- All Passes must be rugby passes, no passes over head height.

- Passes can go in any direction.

- The team in possession can use the end zone player of the opposition as an extra man, but he cannot leave the End Zone.

- Players can run in possession but possession goes to the other team if they are touched.

- First team to score 10 points wins.

PLAYERS	2 Teams
WHAT DO YOU NEED?	1 Ball, 8 Cones,
GRID SIZE	10m x 20m

◯	Ball	
⊗	Player	
◠	Bag	
▭	Shield	
- - - - -➤	Kick/Roll	
·········➤	Run Without a Ball	
────➤	Pass	
────➤	Run With a Ball	
△	Cone/Marker	

Explanation

- The rules are similar to END ZONE.

- However to score the attackers must run the ball through the End Zone and over the endline.

- The attackers "End Zone" defender e.g. X, for the X's can come into play when his team are in possession but must remain in the End Zone when defending.

- No other defenders can go in the End Zone except the nominated player.

- First team to score 10 points wins.

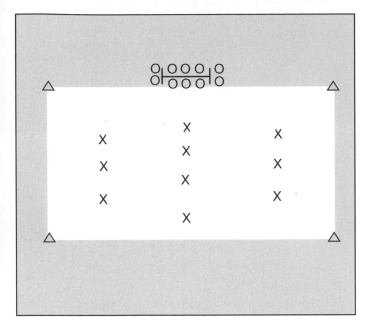

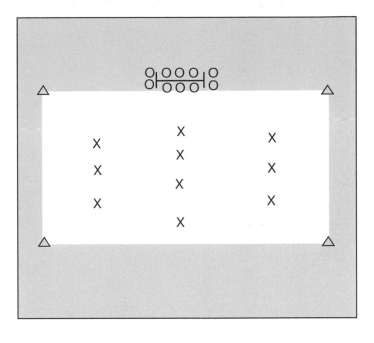

PLAYERS	2 Teams
WHAT DO YOU NEED?	1 Ball, 4 Cones,
GRID SIZE	Half a Pitch

◯	Ball
⊗	Player
⌂	Bag
▭	Shield
------->	Kick/Roll
·········>	Run Without a Ball
———>	Pass
———>	Run With a Ball
△	Cone/Marker

PLAYERS	2 Teams
WHAT DO YOU NEED?	1 Ball, 4 Cones,
GRID SIZE	Half a Pitch

◯	Ball
⊗	Player
⌂	Bag
▭	Shield
------->	Kick/Roll
·········>	Run Without a Ball
———>	Pass
———>	Run With a Ball
△	Cone/Marker

Explanation

- Split the players into 2 teams.
- The defenders stand in a group behind the posts.
- One defender has the ball and he kicks the ball anywhere in the top half of the field.
- If the ball goes over the side lines or half way on the full the attack get an automatic score of 1 point.
- The ball must go at least 20m forwards or again the attack get an automatic score of 1 point.
- The one defender follows his kick and the attackers get 'one' play to score.
- If successful they get 1 point.
- The 2 defenders repeat the act, but the attack gets 2 plays to score, 3 defenders, 3 plays and so -on.
- Normal touch and pass rules are used knock-ons, forward passes etc i.e. 2 handed touch and ball carrier goes to ground, regains his feet and rolls the ball back through his legs to restart play.
- If the attack fails to score on 2 occasions, roles are reversed and the defenders become the attackers.
- Each team has 3 attacking innings.
- The team with the most points wins.

Explanation

- As with 'Against the odds'.
- However each team this time has 6 designated attacks, before changing roles with the defenders.
- On each kick out by the defenders the coach nominates the number of defenders involved, so if the coach calls 'five' then five defenders follow the kick and the attack has five plays to score.
- The rules are exactly the same
- Each team has 3 lots of 6 attacks
- The winning team has the most points at the end.

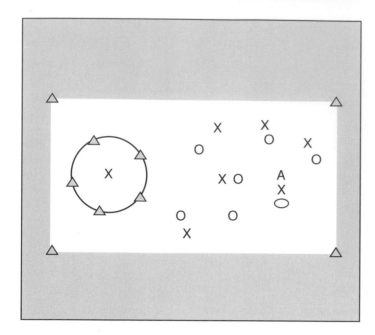

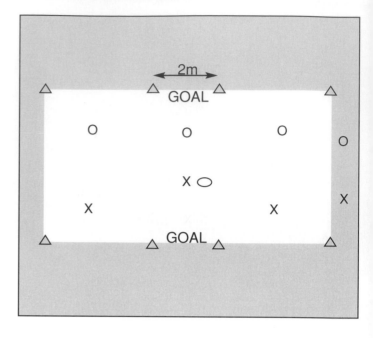

PLAYERS	2 Teams
WHAT DO YOU NEED?	1 Ball, 9 Cones,
GRID SIZE	30m x 60m

⬯	Ball
⊗	Player
⌒	Bag
▭	Shield
- - - - -➔	Kick/Roll
·········➔	Run Without a Ball
——➔	Pass
▭——➔	Run With a Ball
△	Cone/Marker

Explanation

- Split the players into 2 equal teams.
- Team X begin with the ball at point A.
- They have a designated player inside the circle.
- No defenders are allowed inside the circle nor are they allowed to stand around the outside of the circle.
- X's must pass the ball successfully to their player inside the circle to score a point.
- No overhead passes are allowed only rugby passes.
- O's (the defenders) try and intercept the passes to deny the attackers.
- No contact is permitted.
- Players cannot score direct from point A.
- Every score or mistake and the game restarts at point A.
- Each team has 3 minutes to attack.
- The team with the most points wins.

PLAYERS	2 Teams
WHAT DO YOU NEED?	1 Ball, 8 Cones,
GRID SIZE	12m x 12m

⬯	Ball
⊗	Player
⌒	Bag
▭	Shield
- - - - -➔	Kick/Roll
·········➔	Run Without a Ball
——➔	Pass
▭——➔	Run With a Ball
△	Cone/Marker

Explanation

- The players are split into 2 teams of 4.
- One player on each team is an interchangable reserve who can come on at any time.
- Each team has a dedicated goalie who is the only player who can defend their goal
- The players can pass in any direction.
- They can run with the ball but must stop and pass when touched.
- 3 touches and handover.
- Any mistake (i.e. drop ball, bad pass) is a handover
- To score the attackers must pass the ball through the oppositions goal line with a rugby style pass.
- Shoot and miss is a hand-over
- Score and the scorers retain possession but attack the opposite way.
- The game is played for 3 minutes.

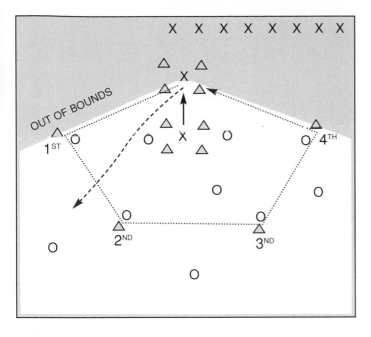

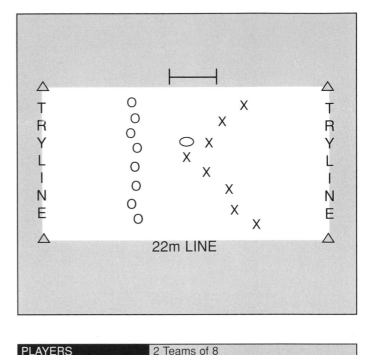

PLAYERS	2 Teams
WHAT DO YOU NEED?	1 Ball, 12 Cones,
GRID SIZE	Half a field

⬭	Ball
⊗	Player
⌓	Bag
▭	Shield
------>	Kick/Roll
·······>	Run Without a Ball
——>	Pass
——>	Run With a Ball
△	Cone/Marker

PLAYERS	2 Teams of 8
WHAT DO YOU NEED?	1 Ball, 4 Cones, 4 Red bibs, 4 Blue bibs
GRID SIZE	12m x 22m line

⬭	Ball
⊗	Player
⌓	Bag
▭	Shield
------>	Kick/Roll
·······>	Run Without a Ball
——>	Pass
——>	Run With a Ball
△	Cone/Marker

Explanation

- The rules are similar to baseball/rounders.
- Split the players into 2 equal teams Team X batters, team O are fielders.
- The batters are fed the ball by one of their own players in the square facing them.
- On catching the pass from the feeder the 'batter' kicks the ball into the field of play.
- He then attempts to run around the bases to get back home.
- The fielders can have two charge down players, if they wish, who once a pass is made to the kicker can run from behind the passing square and try to block the kick.
- The fielders try and collect the kicks and get it to a 'base' before the batsman gets there, or a player is touched with the ball between bases.
- A player is out if his kick goes out of bounds, his kick is caught on the full, his kick is blocked by the 'charge down', if the ball is touched on the base he is running to, before he gets there.
- A player can stop on any base on his way round but will only score a point when he gets home.
- A player getting all the way around in one go scores 5 points.
- Each team has 5 innings, each time 3 players are out the innings is over.
- The ball is dead when its back in the bowlers hands.

Explanation

- The game is played across the field inside the 22m area.
- The players are split into 2 teams of 8 (X attackers, O defenders).
- The attackers are given the ball on their own try line and they attack for 3 minutes.
- Each time they make a mistake (knock-on etc) they start again from their own line.
- The defenders are given coloured bibs (in this case red and blue).
- The game is played under normal 'touch' rules i.e. tackled player goes to ground - regains his feet and rolls the ball back through his legs to restart the game.
- It is 2 handed touch.
- At anytime however during the 3 mins the coach can call out red or blue, the players wearing that coloured bib must run and touch the sideline before coming back into play.
- The onus is on the attack to exploit the spaces.
- 1 point for each try scored, team with most points after both teams have attacked and defended wins.

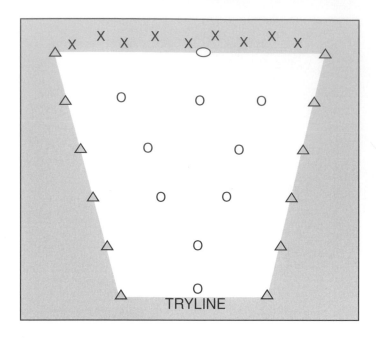

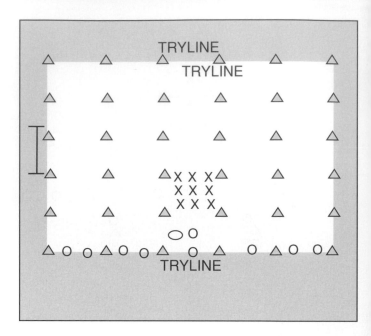

PLAYERS	2 Teams
WHAT DO YOU NEED?	1 Ball, 12 Cones,
GRID SIZE	50m length, narrowing from 25m - 10m

⬭	Ball
⊗	Player
⌒	Bag
▭	Shield
- - - - ->	Kick/Roll
·········>	Run Without a Ball
———>	Pass
———>	Run With a Ball
△	Cone/Marker

PLAYERS	2 Teams
WHAT DO YOU NEED?	1 Ball, 36 Cones
GRID SIZE	Half of pitch playing accross the field

⬭	Ball
⊗	Player
⌒	Bag
▭	Shield
- - - - ->	Kick/Roll
·········>	Run Without a Ball
———>	Pass
———>	Run With a Ball
△	Cone/Marker

Explanation

- Split the players into 2 equal teams Team X attackers, team O are defenders.
- The defenders split their team as in the diagram, the grid begins very wide and funnels down to a narrow try line.
- The defenders can only move forwards and CANNOT CHASE BACK.
- The attackers try to beat the defenders as they move down the narrowing grid to score over the try-line at the bottom.
- They have five attempts to score before the teams switch roles.
- The team which scores the most tries wins.

Explanation

- The game is played across the field using either half or a full pitch but play using the touchlines as the trylines.
- Split the field into 5 equal zones (as shown).
- Split the players into two equal teams, one team (O) will attack for 3 minutes and the other team (X) will defend before changing roles.
- The attacking team has 'unlimited' touch during their 3 minutes. If they make a mistake (knock-on etc.) they begin again from their own line.
- The game has NO kicking but is played under usual touch rules.
- A player 'touched' in possession must lay on the ground until ALL the defenders congregate in the zone the tackle is made in i.e. all the other zones are empty of defenders only then may the attack play the ball away leaving the defenders to slide hard to close them down.
- After 1 minute allow the defenders to have one nominated player who can stand/defend in any zone but all the rest must be in the zone where the player is tackled.
- During the third minute, wherever a tackle/touch is made, again all defenders must congregate in the zone the tackle is 'effected' but they are allowed to have one defender in each of the other four zones.
- The team that scores the most tries wins.
- The regulations of where to stand are only in force until the ball comes into play then the defenders can run and stand anywhere on the field.

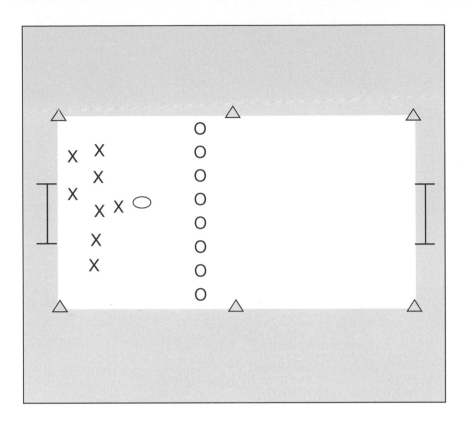

PLAYERS	2 Teams

WHAT DO YOU NEED?	1 Ball, 6 Cones,

GRID SIZE	Full Field (dependant on No. of players)

◯	Ball
⊗	Player
◠	Bag
▭	Shield
- - - -►	Kick/Roll
·········►	Run Without a Ball
──►	Pass
──►	Run With a Ball
△	Cone/Marker

Explanation

- Split the players into 2 equal teams Team X attackers, team O are defenders.
- The attacking team begins with the ball 20m from their own line.
- NO kicking is allowed.
- The attackers have unlimited tackles.
- Defenders must use 2 handed touch.
- When an attacker is touched they must go onto both knees, regain their feet and roll the ball through their legs to bring it back into play.
- On each tackle a defender MUST leave the pitch, which gradually gives a numeric advantage to the attack.

- The attack has 4 minutes to score as many tries as possible.
- Every score allows the defenders to come back on and start on equal terms
- The attackers simply attack in the other direction from 20m out from their own line.
- Each time the attack makes a mistake (forward pass etc) the game is restarted at the 20m line and all the defenders come back into play.
- Both teams have 4 minutes to attack, the team with the most scores wins.

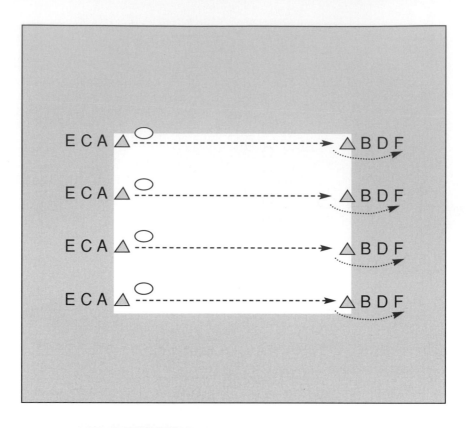

PLAYERS	4 Teams
WHAT DO YOU NEED?	4 Balls, 8 Cones
GRID SIZE	Varies on number of players and space

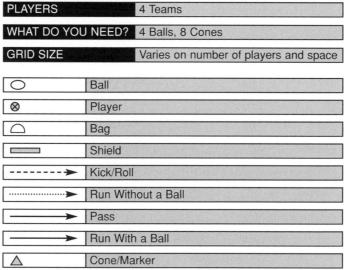

○	Ball
⊗	Player
⌂	Bag
▭	Shield
- - - - - -►	Kick/Roll
·············►	Run Without a Ball
———————►	Pass
———————►	Run With a Ball
△	Cone/Marker

When you're stuck for equipment, space or even sometimes numbers relays are a great way of keeping a group occupied, practicing basic skills and just having fun.

It's amazing what can be achieved with a bit of thought and imagination you can do relays against the clock if you're short of numbers or in different teams if you have lots of players.

The following relays are in two lines one at each end where the winning team will have its players back in their original position first.

Each of the following has player A, running to player B – to player C etc. until everyone is back where they began.

Explanation

- Run and hand on (to the next player).

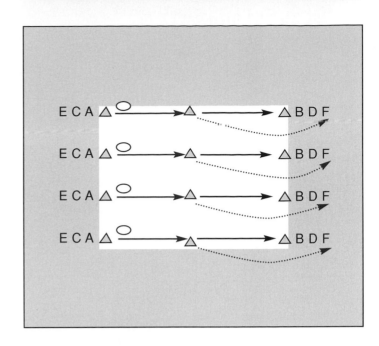

TWO LINE RELAYS 2

PLAYERS	4 Teams
WHAT DO YOU NEED?	1 Ball, 8 Cones
GRID SIZE	Varies on number of players and space

○	Ball
⊗	Player
◠	Bag
▭	Shield
------>	Kick/Roll
········>	Run Without a Ball
———>	Pass
———>	Run With a Ball
△	Cone/Marker

Explanation

- Run and pass on (to the next player) from anywhere.

TWO LINE RELAYS 3

PLAYERS	4 Teams
WHAT DO YOU NEED?	1 Ball, 12 Cones
GRID SIZE	Varies on number of players and space

○	Ball
⊗	Player
◠	Bag
▭	Shield
------>	Kick/Roll
········>	Run Without a Ball
———>	Pass
———>	Run With a Ball
△	Cone/Marker

Explanation

- Run and pass on (to the next player) from half way.

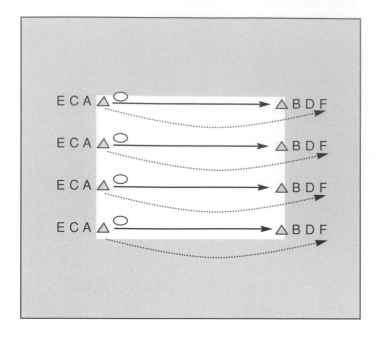

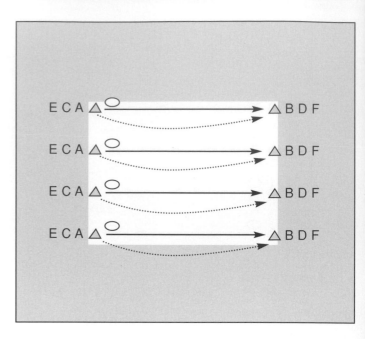

PLAYERS	4 Teams
WHAT DO YOU NEED?	1 Ball, 8 Cones
GRID SIZE	Varies on number of players and space

◯	Ball
⊗	Player
◠	Bag
▭	Shield
- - - - ▸	Kick/Roll
·········▸	Run Without a Ball
——▸	Pass
——▸	Run With a Ball
△	Cone/Marker

Explanation

• Pass (to the next player) and run.

PLAYERS	4 Teams
WHAT DO YOU NEED?	1 Ball, 12 Cones
GRID SIZE	Varies on number of players and space

◯	Ball
⊗	Player
◠	Bag
▭	Shield
- - - - ▸	Kick/Roll
·········▸	Run Without a Ball
——▸	Pass
——▸	Run With a Ball
△	Cone/Marker

Explanation

• Pass from the ground and run (same as 53 but receiver must place the ball at his feet until the passer has tagged him).

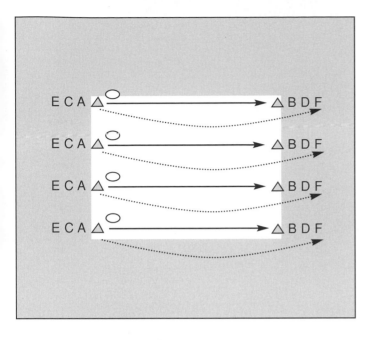

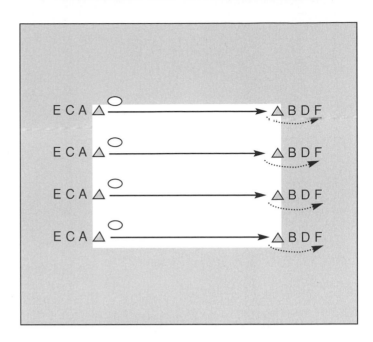

PLAYERS	4 Teams
WHAT DO YOU NEED?	1 Ball, 8 Cones
GRID SIZE	Varies on number of players and space

⬭	Ball
⊗	Player
⌒	Bag
▭	Shield
------→	Kick/Roll
·······→	Run Without a Ball
———→	Pass
———→	Run With a Ball
△	Cone/Marker

Explanation
- Overhead pass (like a soccer throw in) and run.

PLAYERS	4 Teams
WHAT DO YOU NEED?	1 Ball, 12 Cones
GRID SIZE	Varies on number of players and space

⬭	Ball
⊗	Player
⌒	Bag
▭	Shield
------→	Kick/Roll
·······→	Run Without a Ball
———→	Pass
———→	Run With a Ball
△	Cone/Marker

Explanation
- Run backwards and hand on.

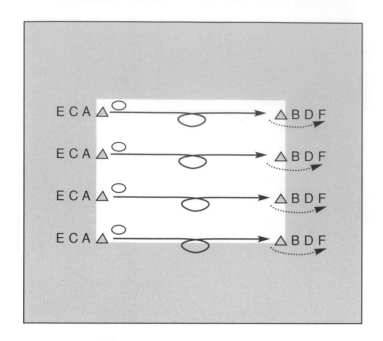

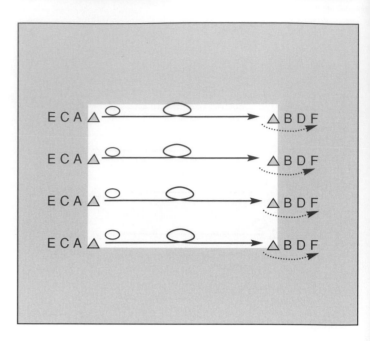

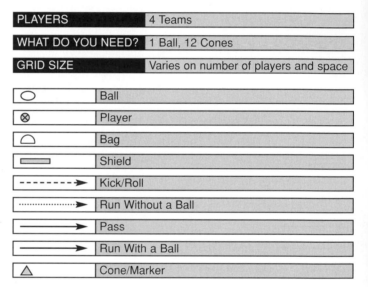

PLAYERS	4 Teams
WHAT DO YOU NEED?	1 Ball, 8 Cones
GRID SIZE	Varies on number of players and space

Symbol	Meaning
◯	Ball
⊗	Player
◠	Bag
▭	Shield
- - - - - ▸	Kick/Roll
⋯⋯⋯▸	Run Without a Ball
——▸	Pass
——▸	Run With a Ball
△	Cone/Marker

Explanation
- Run, spin right and hand on.

PLAYERS	4 Teams
WHAT DO YOU NEED?	1 Ball, 12 Cones
GRID SIZE	Varies on number of players and space

Symbol	Meaning
◯	Ball
⊗	Player
◠	Bag
▭	Shield
- - - - - ▸	Kick/Roll
⋯⋯⋯▸	Run Without a Ball
——▸	Pass
——▸	Run With a Ball
△	Cone/Marker

Explanation
- Run, spin left and hand on.

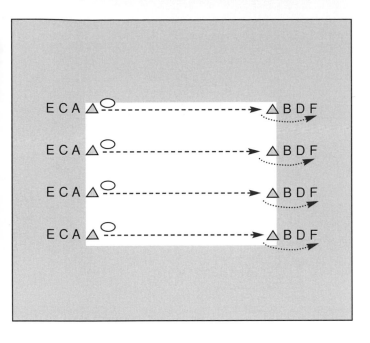

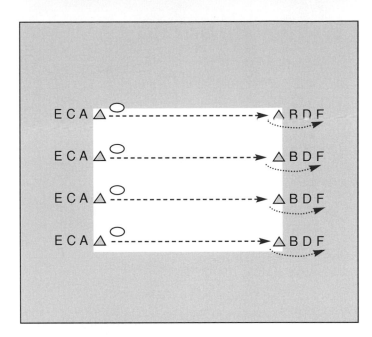

PLAYERS	4 Teams
WHAT DO YOU NEED?	4 Balls, 8 Cones
GRID SIZE	Varies on number of players and space

⬭	Ball
⊗	Player
⌂	Bag
▭	Shield
- - - - ->	Kick/Roll
·······>	Run Without a Ball
——>	Pass
——>	Run With a Ball
△	Cone/Marker

Explanation

• Dribble the ball, pick-up and hand on.

PLAYERS	4 Teams
WHAT DO YOU NEED?	4 Balls, 8 Cones
GRID SIZE	Varies on number of players and space

⬭	Ball
⊗	Player
⌂	Bag
▭	Shield
- - - - ->	Kick/Roll
·······>	Run Without a Ball
——>	Pass
——>	Run With a Ball
△	Cone/Marker

Explanation

• Dribble the ball no hands.

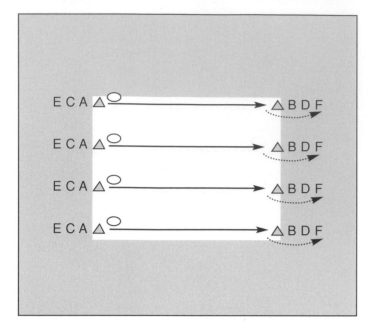

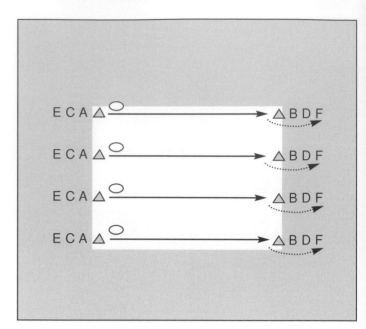

PLAYERS	4 Teams
WHAT DO YOU NEED?	4 Balls, 8 Cones
GRID SIZE	Varies on number of players and space

◯	Ball
⊗	Player
◠	Bag
▭	Shield
--------►	Kick/Roll
·········►	Run Without a Ball
───►	Pass
───►	Run With a Ball
△	Cone/Marker

Explanation
● Figure 8 (whilst moving across the space - figure 8 through the legs).

PLAYERS	4 Teams
WHAT DO YOU NEED?	4 Balls, 8 Cones
GRID SIZE	Varies on number of players and space

◯	Ball
⊗	Player
◠	Bag
▭	Shield
--------►	Kick/Roll
·········►	Run Without a Ball
───►	Pass
───►	Run With a Ball
△	Cone/Marker

Explanation
● Pass the ball around the waist (Left and right) and hand on.

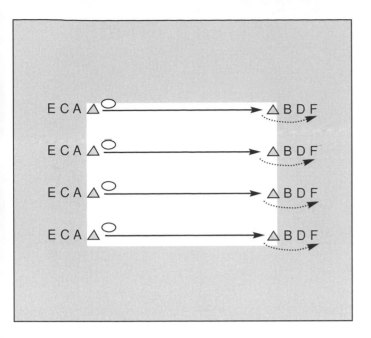

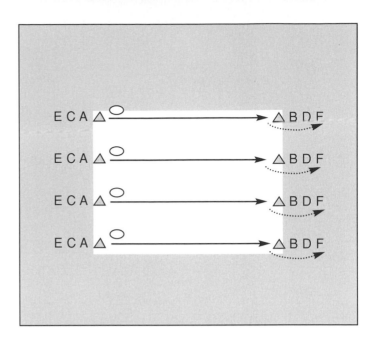

PLAYERS	4 Teams
WHAT DO YOU NEED?	4 Balls, 8 Cones
GRID SIZE	Varies on number of players and space

○	Ball
⊗	Player
⌒	Bag
▭	Shield
- - - - - - ▶	Kick/Roll
·············▶	Run Without a Ball
——————▶	Pass
——————▶	Run With a Ball
△	Cone/Marker

Explanation

• Around the knees and hand on.

PLAYERS	4 Teams
WHAT DO YOU NEED?	4 Balls, 8 Cones
GRID SIZE	Varies on number of players and space

○	Ball
⊗	Player
⌒	Bag
▭	Shield
- - - - - - ▶	Kick/Roll
·············▶	Run Without a Ball
——————▶	Pass
——————▶	Run With a Ball
△	Cone/Marker

Explanation

• Bounce (at least four times) and hand on.

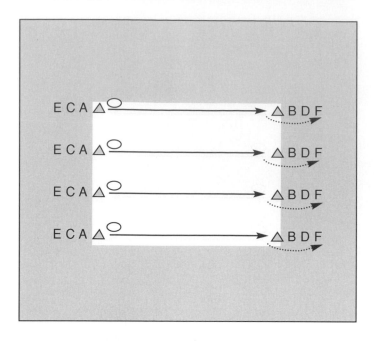

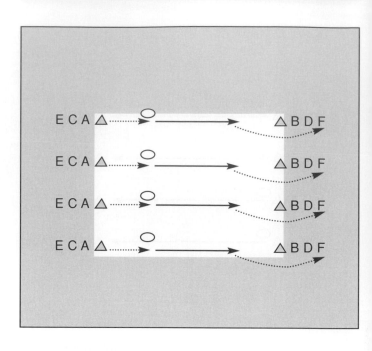

PLAYERS	4 Teams
WHAT DO YOU NEED?	4 Balls, 8 Cones
GRID SIZE	Varies on number of players and space

⬭	Ball
⊗	Player
⌓	Bag
▭	Shield
--------►	Kick/Roll
·········►	Run Without a Ball
——►	Pass
——►	Run With a Ball
△	Cone/Marker

Explanation

• Headers (at least four times) and hand on.

PLAYERS	4 Teams
WHAT DO YOU NEED?	4 Balls, 8 Cones
GRID SIZE	Varies on number of players and space

⬭	Ball
⊗	Player
⌓	Bag
▭	Shield
--------►	Kick/Roll
·········►	Run Without a Ball
——►	Pass
——►	Run With a Ball
△	Cone/Marker

Explanation

• Pick-up and put down

• Ball is placed 3m from A who runs picks it up and places it down 3m from B who repeats.

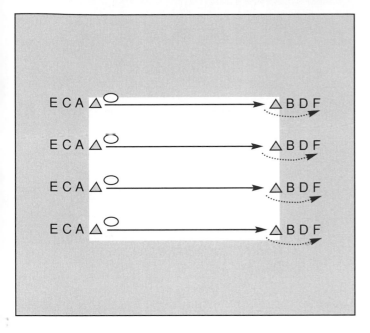

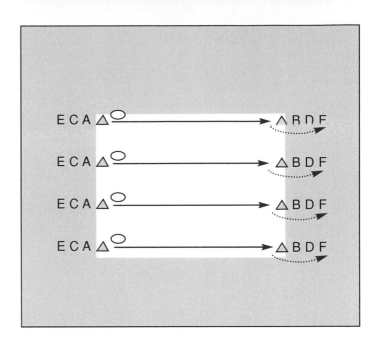

PLAYERS	4 Teams
WHAT DO YOU NEED?	4 Balls, 8 Cones
GRID SIZE	Varies on number of players and space

◯	Ball
⊗	Player
◠	Bag
▭	Shield
- - - - - ▶	Kick/Roll
········▶	Run Without a Ball
———▶	Pass
———▶	Run With a Ball
△	Cone/Marker

Explanation

• Around the head and hand off.

PLAYERS	4 Teams
WHAT DO YOU NEED?	4 Balls, 8 Cones
GRID SIZE	Varies on number of players and space

◯	Ball
⊗	Player
◠	Bag
▭	Shield
- - - - - ▶	Kick/Roll
········▶	Run Without a Ball
———▶	Pass
———▶	Run With a Ball
△	Cone/Marker

Explanation

• Around the ankles and hand off.

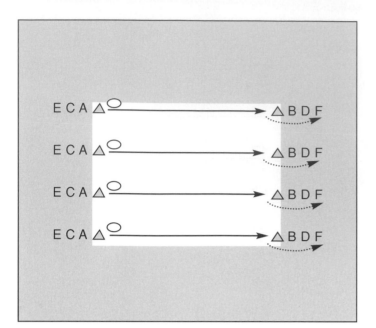

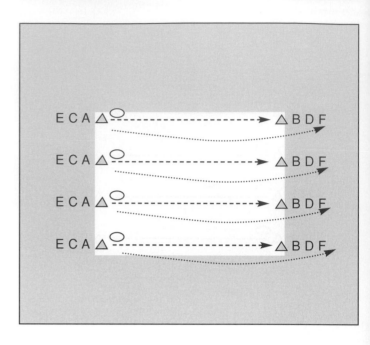

PLAYERS	4 Teams
WHAT DO YOU NEED?	4 Balls, 8 Cones
GRID SIZE	Varies on number of players and space

⬭	Ball
⊗	Player
⌂	Bag
▭	Shield
-------→	Kick/Roll
·······→	Run Without a Ball
——→	Pass
——→	Run With a Ball
△	Cone/Marker

Explanation
- Around the head juggle and hand off.

PLAYERS	4 Teams
WHAT DO YOU NEED?	4 Balls, 8 Cones
GRID SIZE	Varies on number of players and space

⬭	Ball
⊗	Player
⌂	Bag
▭	Shield
-------→	Kick/Roll
·······→	Run Without a Ball
——→	Pass
——→	Run With a Ball
△	Cone/Marker

Explanation
- Chip kick to player B and follow.

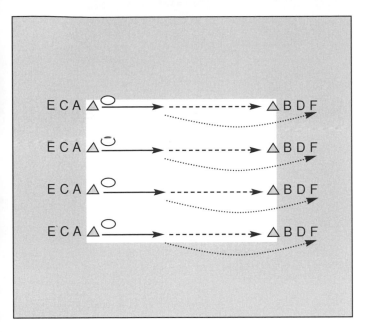

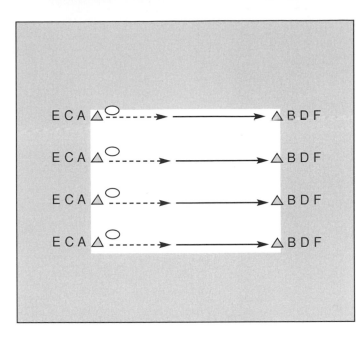

PLAYERS	4 Teams
WHAT DO YOU NEED?	4 Balls, 8 Cones
GRID SIZE	Varies on number of players and space

○	Ball
⊗	Player
△	Bag
▭	Shield
- - - - ➤	Kick/Roll
·········➤	Run Without a Ball
——➤	Pass
——➤	Run With a Ball
△	Cone/Marker

Explanation
- Player A runs and grubber kicks to player B who catches and repeats.

PLAYERS	4 Teams
WHAT DO YOU NEED?	4 Balls, 8 Cones
GRID SIZE	Varies on number of players and space

○	Ball
⊗	Player
△	Bag
▭	Shield
- - - - ➤	Kick/Roll
·········➤	Run Without a Ball
——➤	Pass
——➤	Run With a Ball
△	Cone/Marker

Explanation
- Kick and pass.
- Player A chips for himself and passes to player B.

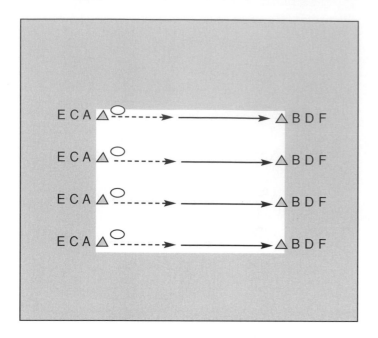

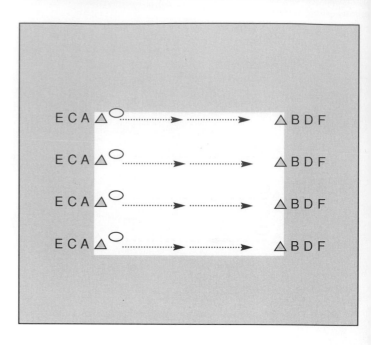

PLAYERS	4 Teams
WHAT DO YOU NEED?	4 Balls, 8 Cones
GRID SIZE	Varies on number of players and space

⬭	Ball
⊗	Player
⌓	Bag
▭	Shield
- - - - - →	Kick/Roll
········→	Run Without a Ball
—→	Pass
——→	Run With a Ball
△	Cone/Marker

Explanation
- Kick and pass 2.
- Player A grubber kicks for himself and passes to player B.

PLAYERS	4 Teams
WHAT DO YOU NEED?	4 Balls, 8 Cones
GRID SIZE	Varies on number of players and space

⬭	Ball
⊗	Player
⌓	Bag
▭	Shield
- - - - - →	Kick/Roll
········→	Run Without a Ball
—→	Pass
——→	Run With a Ball
△	Cone/Marker

Explanation
- Toss and catch.
- Player A throws up and catches whilst crossing to player B.
- He MUST NOT run in possession.

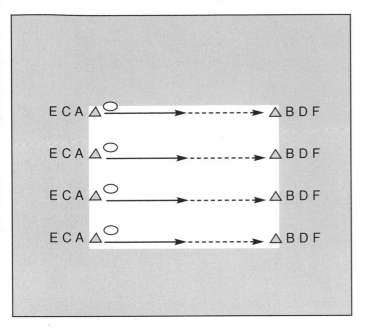

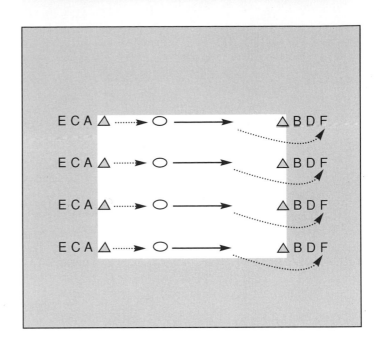

PLAYERS	4 Teams
WHAT DO YOU NEED?	4 Balls, 8 Cones
GRID SIZE	Varies on number of players and space

◯	Ball
⊗	Player
◠	Bag
▭	Shield
- - - - ▸	Kick/Roll
⋯⋯⋯▸	Run Without a Ball
———▸	Pass
———▸	Run With a Ball
△	Cone/Marker

Explanation
- Roll the ball.
- Player A runs with ball to half-way and then rolls it to player B.
- Who must collect it and repeat.

PLAYERS	4 Teams
WHAT DO YOU NEED?	4 Balls, 8 Cones
GRID SIZE	Varies on number of players and space

◯	Ball
⊗	Player
◠	Bag
▭	Shield
- - - - ▸	Kick/Roll
⋯⋯⋯▸	Run Without a Ball
———▸	Pass
———▸	Run With a Ball
△	Cone/Marker

Explanation
- Dive on the ball.
- A ball is placed 3m infront of player A.
- Player A must run and dive on the ball, regain his feet and place the ball 3m from player B who repeats.

- For a more advanced skill get the players to roll the ball infront of themselves to dive on.

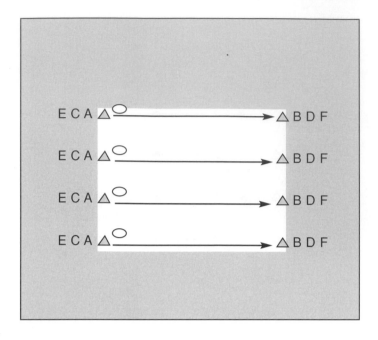

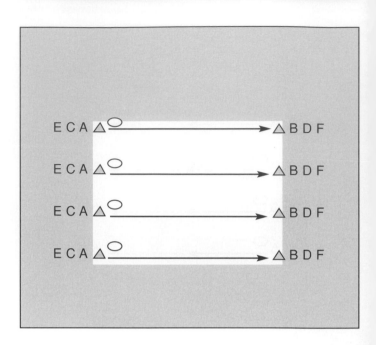

PLAYERS	4 Teams
WHAT DO YOU NEED?	4 Balls, 8 Cones
GRID SIZE	Varies on number of players and space

⬭	Ball
⊗	Player
⌂	Bag
▭	Shield
- - - - - ▸	Kick/Roll
········▸	Run Without a Ball
——▸	Pass
——▸	Run With a Ball
△	Cone/Marker

Explanation

- Pass and sit
- Player A passes to player B and sits down.
- Player B catches the ball and passes to player c and sits down.
- This is repeated until the last player is has the ball.

PLAYERS	4 Teams
WHAT DO YOU NEED?	4 Balls, 8 Cones
GRID SIZE	Varies on number of players and space

⬭	Ball
⊗	Player
⌂	Bag
▭	Shield
- - - - - ▸	Kick/Roll
········▸	Run Without a Ball
——▸	Pass
——▸	Run With a Ball
△	Cone/Marker

Explanation

- Stand, Catch and pass.
- As 28 but with all players sitting on the ground except the last man.
- Players stand as the ball is passed to them.

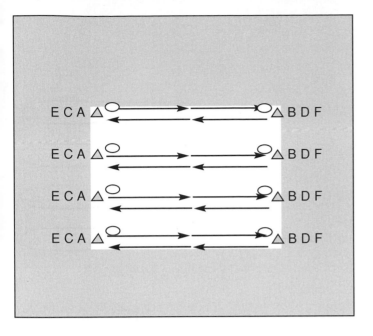

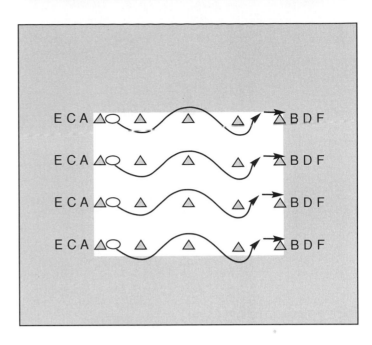

PLAYERS	4 Teams
WHAT DO YOU NEED?	8 Balls, 8 Cones
GRID SIZE	Varies on number of players and space

◯	Ball
⊗	Player
◠	Bag
▭	Shield
- - - - →	Kick/Roll
·········→	Run Without a Ball
——→	Pass
——→	Run With a Ball
△	Cone/Marker

Explanation
- 2 ball relay.
- Player A runs and passes to player D.
- At the same time player B runs and passes to player C.

PLAYERS	4 Teams
WHAT DO YOU NEED?	4 Balls, 20 Cones
GRID SIZE	Varies on number of players and space

◯	Ball
⊗	Player
◠	Bag
▭	Shield
- - - - →	Kick/Roll
·········→	Run Without a Ball
——→	Pass
——→	Run With a Ball
△	Cone/Marker

Explanation
- Weaver.
- Cones are placed between the lines of players.
- The players must weave in and out of the cones before handing off the the next player.

Extension
- 2 handed carry.
- Behind the back carry.
- On the head carry.
- Right arm carry.
- Left arm carry.

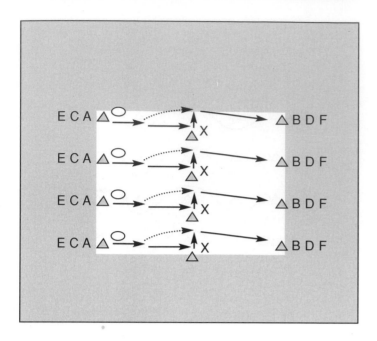
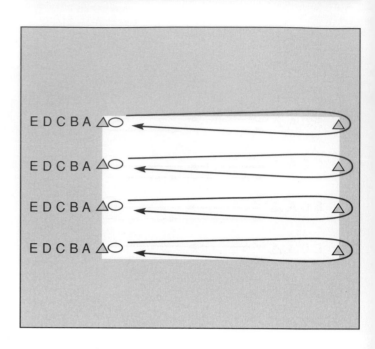

PLAYERS	4 Teams
WHAT DO YOU NEED?	8 Balls, 12 Cones
GRID SIZE	Varies on number of players and space

⬭	Ball
⊗	Player
⌒	Bag
▭	Shield
- - - - - ▸	Kick/Roll
·········▸	Run Without a Ball
———▸	Pass
———▸	Run With a Ball
△	Cone/Marker

PLAYERS	4 Teams
WHAT DO YOU NEED?	4 Balls, 8 Cones
GRID SIZE	Varies on number of players and space

⬭	Ball
⊗	Player
⌒	Bag
▭	Shield
- - - - - ▸	Kick/Roll
·········▸	Run Without a Ball
———▸	Pass
———▸	Run With a Ball
△	Cone/Marker

Explanation

- A player (X) is placed in the middle of the 2 lines on a cone
- Player A runs and passes to him
- X receives the pass and passes back to the player A.
- Player A runs on and passes to player B who repeats.
- This can be done using a variety of the exercise in numbers 1-27.

Explanation

- The activities mentioned in the 2 line relays are just as suitable here, but there is more space for the players to practice their skills.
- In these relays the players run to the cone opposite and return before handing to the next player.
- You can combine skills or use them alongside any number of agility drills.
- As with all drills, games and practices the only limit is your imagination, I'm sure there are many other skills you can include or adapt.